The Voices We Hear Daily

Fr. Eugene Azorji

En Route Books and Media, LLC
Saint Louis, MO

⊕*ENROUTE*
Make the time

En Route Books and Media, LLC

5705 Rhodes Avenue

St. Louis, MO 63109

Contact us at **contact@enroutebooksandmedia.com**

Cover Credit: Sebastian Mahfood

ISBN-13: 979-8-88870-139-3

Library of Congress Control Number: 2024932418

Dedication

This book is dedicated to
Mr. and Mrs. Joe and Dorothy Hafertepe,
Audery Jackson, and Gabriel and Agnes Azorji

Table of Contents

Foreword

The Very Reverend Eugene Azorji has dedicated over 30 years of his priestly ministry to the formation of many seminarians across ages and cultures as they discern their vocations. I am a beneficiary of the author's vast experiences and wisdom.

This reflection on Vocational Discernment is so timely. Ours is a challenging time when the youth especially face and hear a plethora of confusing and conflicting voices. Discernment may also be useful to people of all affiliations seeking a purposeful and meaningful life.

In *The Voices We Hear Daily*, the author helps readers to explore various ways to seek sound discernment for their states in life to align them to the core of their being. When those searching for vocations to the Priesthood and Religious life discern well, respond in faith, and listen to God, they savor opportunities for being in communion with creation and Creator.

Fr. Eugene Okoli PhD
Pastoral Administrator
St Gabriel's Catholic Church
McKinney Texas

Introduction

The voice of God created the universe: It was the voice of God through the voice of the archangel that a child was conceived, the son of God, the "true image of the invisible God"; the voice of God through the voices of the Apostles that the church came into being. That same voice of God speaks to us today, through the church, through the sacraments, and through bearing witness to the gospel. That same voice is loud and clear, but the voice of self, the world, and the devil make it harder today for people to hear the true voice of God. It is through discernment that people discover the true voice of God, and where God is directing each of us. There is a universal invitation by God to Holiness, an invitation that requires an act of faith. This faith is a response to God's invitation, and it implies trust, conviction, and commitment. When you hear the voice of God, "harden not your heart."

Vocational discernment is an art of choosing well. There are varieties of vocations and states of life. My emphasis here is about priestly or religious vocations. Married or unmarried states of life are also vocations of their own merit. The goal of each vocation is to fulfill God's plan for each state of life for each person and most importantly to gain eternal life. My focus in this book is about young people aspiring to the priesthood and grappling with the issues of decision-making. In this context, they hear about things, ideas, people, and the world. They are confused, disorganized, disoriented, and vulnerable. They need a guide and a sense of direction to make wise and useful choices concerning their respective vocations in life.

Writing a book is like building a new house. A person who wants to build a new house must make sure all the essential elements for the house are available. He must have the materials and financial resources to start and finish the project. In detail, he must make sure he has the "property" on which the house is to be built. He must also make sure he has other collateral investment to rely upon when the financial resources appear to dry up. When these items are ready, he must make sure that he has a blueprint of the house. This design will show what type of house, what model of house, and what number of rooms and facilities are contained in the new house. After getting the materials ready, he will look for experts in building construction. He will lay out the structural foundation perhaps with concrete and iron and do the concrete flooring before the blocks are erected. This process will take time and money, but it also requires some things on the part of the builder, namely diligence, patience, and good planning.

The same process can be said of writing a book. The author must have a topic which he wants to discuss as he lays out the ideas of the topic in an organized fashion, such as the chapters, and sub-chapters in a format that is generally accepted by publishers. The author must also consider his immediate audience and perhaps outside audiences that may benefit from the book. The topic of writing must be clear and distinct and must express the content of the book, showing vividly the authors' way of communicating his message to the public.

The motivation behind the writing of this book is based on my many years in the seminary as a teacher, formator/spiritual director. I have been in formation houses for over thirty years and have learned firsthand the unique personalities of seminarians. I can predict safely the positive and negative signs of a seminarian discerning priesthood. The Holy Spirit, however, oversees every discernment, but there are basic human elements that demonstrate that a student is ready to be formed or not.

From my experience as a spiritual director, I have come to conclude that almost all those I have helped in their spiritual journey share unique stories of their spiritual life and that "they hear every day, four voices namely, the voice of God, the voice of the world, the voice of self, and the voice of the Devil."

So, I have designed this book to reflect on the voices we hear every day. This can also be applied to the secular world. Having been raised in the Thomistic tradition, I was tempted to delve into definitions of terms like "What is voice" or "the self" or "the devil" or "the world," but I would rather refer the reader to other sources for their explanation. So, my style in this book is a simple narrative, a spiritual journey, though rough in some places, but it is refreshing and inspiring by many counts.

The Scripture teaches us that Faith comes from hearing, and hearing the word of God and keeping it is like building a house on a strong foundation (rock) so that when the rain and wind come, it stands unshaken to the ground. The ear is therefore the organ of Faith. But the ear hears a lot—the good, the bad, and the ugly. The body part "ear" is that powerful organ that enables us to hear of things around us. Through our ears, we hear the voices of our parents, our teachers, our friends, and significant others. We also hear bad things with our ears, such as bad news, gossip, nasty stories about hate and crimes around us. The ear hears it all, but paradoxically, the ear is the last of the vital organs in our body to die. When my mother passed away in 2007, I knew she had died when she was unable to hear her name as I called her "MOM Agnes". There is always a relationship between the ear and the brain, and the ear coordinates the brain, speech, and respiratory organs so well that what affects one affects the other. Persons with hearing impairment do experience problems of communication and interpersonal skills. One of the important miracles of Jesus was to make the deaf and dumb able to hear and speak. Hearing and speaking the word of God is like theory and practice in our daily lives. The voices we hear each day are about life encounters we experience with the self, the world, the devil, and God in this "valley of tears" and how we overcome some of these challenges through God's grace and magnanimity. Sometimes we think that life is linear, but often it is rather undulating. When God spoke through the mouth of the prophet Jeremiah, "if you hear his voice today, do not harden your hearts," he was indirectly speaking to us. Many times, we hear God's voice, through varieties of media, and still, we remain cold, unmoved, unperturbed, unruffled, and apathetic to the voice of God. God speaks to us every day, but it is through the ears of faith that we can discern properly that "yes, God is speaking to me today through this medium." There are waves of voices today coming from all angles, but through discernment, you can safely dictate the voices of self, of the world, of the devil and of God, coming simultaneously to an individual who seem to be at "a crossroads of life." Sometimes, these voices are mixed up and messed up so that it becomes very difficult for the individual to make choices about the right way to go. Among the questions that are before us to ask are these: what are these voices like, how do they come to us, and why do they come the way they come, complicated and sometimes shrouded in mystery? Let us study in a more detailed format what the voices of self might look like in the real world.

Chapter 1

The Voice of Self

The opening chapters of the book of Genesis give us an idea of the voices of self, right away! The dignity of the human person was first accorded to man by God when he created man and woman in his own image and likeness. The dignity was distorted by man himself when he listened to his own voice, and of course the voice of the devil, to disobey God. The consequence of this disobedience is suffering, toil, pain, and death. This original tendency to listen to the voice of self instead of the voice of God has brought us to where we are today. The rest is history. The summary of this history is the classical definition of Original Sin. Thus, we have human conditions of suffering, pain, temptation, and death.

Human psychology has taught us that "a fully human person preserves a balance between interiority and exteriority. Both the extreme introvert and extreme extrovert are off balance" (Powell, *Why am I afraid to tell you who I am?*). What this means is that we hear ourselves loudly and clearly, but when we follow the extreme of the voices, we hear about ourselves whether it is within or without the confines of our personhood, then we place self in a position of power, authority, idol, or little god. This was how our first parents derailed. The devil told them that they will be like God knowing the tree of knowledge of good and evil (Gen. 3:5), and, out of pride, they disobeyed God. Powell explains that "[b]alanced introverts hear their voices, but their voices help them to experience and explore who they are." The voice of self is upright and beneficial when it is the voice of God in us. The voice of self helps us know the vi- tality of self, the emotions, senses, mind, and will. The voice of self helps us to know when we are sick, healthy, or pre- occupied with strange feelings. The voice of self in this sense hears no evil and is not afraid of what it hears. The voice of self, seen positively, means, according to Powell, that "you accept yourself the way God wants you to be as a beloved son," and indeed a fully functioning person. The voice of the person who is an extrovert, on the other hand, means that he is open to himself and to the outside world. He hears his own voices and the voices of the world around him with all the emotional and physical implications. Pow- ell describes a voice of self who is extroverted this way:

They are born again in every springtime, feel the im- pact of the great mysteries of life: birth, growth, love, suffering, death. Their hearts skip along with the young lovers, and they know something of the exhilaration that is in them. They also know the ghetto's philosophy of despair, the loneliness of suffering without relief. The bell never tolls without tolling in some strange way for them.

The voice of self that is dangerous comes from the two extremes of those who are introverted or extroverted. This is not to say that those who are well integrated do not exhibit bad behavior or that they do not hear things detrimental to themselves, but to show that "all have sinned and run short of the grace of God."

As I wake up every morning, no matter how healthy or ill I am, I am bedeviled with voices or directions by my thoughts, emotions, and strength on the directions to go throughout the day. My own voice may present to me varieties of choices from which to choose. It might be from what is desirable or undesirable; it might be a temptation to do something right or wrong; it might be what is appetizing to the eye, the ear, or the mouth. The voice of self starts from the basic instinct of self-preservation. The self tries to please itself by satisfying the basic biological needs outlined by Abraham Maslow (e.g., food, safety, relationships, and self-actualization). The self is good because it is the handiwork of God, but the self can rely on itself alone for the day-to-day activities, that is, the self puts itself in deep trouble. The first enemy of self is pride, and pride is the root of the seven cardinal sins. When the self operates on its own power, on its own merit and authority, the voices of self become selfish, arrogant, misleading, crafty, narcistic, self-centered, and earth-bound. A typical example is the story of Moses and Aaron who were leaders of the Israelites on their journey to the promised land. Moses and Aaron were wonderful leaders, but they were denied reaching the promised land because they relied on the power of "self" and not the power of God to carry out his instructions. God asked Moses to "speak" to the rock instead of "strike" the rock. Moses taught that by using human strength, or a power of his own, he could earn the result of providing water to his people. Moses called his people "rebels' because they were too demanding to have water for their families, but, out of frustration, Moses wanted to do "magic" instead of complete surrender to the grace of God. He failed, he struggled, and he did not reach his goal. He was denied reaching the promised land.

This story of Moses reminds us of the sin of disobedience to the voice of God. When God gives instructions on how life is to be approached, we tend to arrogate to ourselves the power to change things contrary to the plan of God. In most of life experiences, we notice that the dictum "Man proposes, but God disposes" is recurrent in today's world. Has it ever occurred to you that many times when you have plans to travel or visit a friend, there and then, you cancel the visit because it is raining or snowing outside? Has it ever occurred to you that many times you may make doctors' appointments, but you couldn't go because there was death in the family or other family challenges more important than the doctor's appointment? The voice of self comes as a contingent plan in our lives, but often we take it as something permanent or eternal. The voice of self is ephemeral, changeable, transient, feeble, fickle, deceptive, and many times not accurate to the realities of the day.

The voice of self is attractive to the senses. This attraction is pleasing to the eye, the ear, the brain, and in fact the whole body to the point where it becomes desirable. When the senses are not disciplined, the voices of self may lead us to inordinate desires. A desire becomes inordinate when the self desires something, an idea, a person for its own sake and not for the sake of God. A desire for self-gratification, self-enjoyment, self-aggrandizement, self-fulfilling is considered an inordinate desire. A few examples of inordinate desires may include the watching of porn, nudity, masturbation, sexual fantasies, and X-rated movies that instigate self -pleasure and self-abuse. Human desire is a human condition and should be channeled appropriately. When desire is pursued for self, it becomes inordinate. When desire is pursued for sake of the kingdom of God, then it fulfills its purpose. Scripture says "seek ye first the kingdom of God, and the rest will be given to you." So, when you desire a thing, an idea, or a person for the sake of self-gratification, it becomes disordered and sinful.

The voice of self comes when one desires to control things, ideas, or people which we call power or greed. The devil was selfish when he took Jesus to the desert to tempt him. "All the earth belongs to me, and I can give it to whoever will obey me and who ever will worship me." The response that Jesus gave him was apt. "Only God alone deserves worship." The voice of self can be manifested in the roles or "games" we play every day. Remember, it is the extremes of these games that stand out as disordered. For instance, Powel teaches that "all heart people follow the heart in all matters, to the point that others wonder if the head is operative at all. The heart decides everything." When John shows soft emotions all the time, the danger is that John may repress the harder emotions and may sometimes snap to undesirable behaviors. Suicidal thoughts like "I am worth nothing," "Nobody likes me," or "I don't have any value anymore" may indicate the roles "all heart" people play. Extremely emotional people are soft and tender and should be handled with care and empathy.

The voice of self comes when one claims to be "Mr. Right." People who show this tendency try to protect their ego by going extra miles to prove that they are right. They cannot concede in any argument because they do not listen to other people's point of view. The danger of this game is the fear, anxiety, and doubt that comes with it. If I am Mr. right, the danger is that I may even doubt myself and what I can do. When the self becomes an idol, the voice of self will worship itself in all kinds of vanities. When a question is asked to a person in this group, like "How are you today?", the voice of self in him will respond, "I look good," "I look handsome," or "I am pretty" if a woman. In other words, the voice of self may lead to self-praise, self-adoration, pride, selfishness, and arrogance. These vices are deadly in themselves. The voice of self may also be expressed by those who want to assert their superiority to others. The voice of self may assume that it has a superior voice or command of every situation to the point where other voices do not matter. But this demonstrates a lack of self-esteem or of prudence. In discerning to the priesthood, the candidate should consider the voice of God and the informed voice of self to make a balanced choice of vocation. The goal of discernment is to make the right choice that is consistent with the will of God for the candidate.

Chapter 2

The Voice of God

In the opening verses of the book to the Hebrews,

God spoke in partial and various ways to our ancestors through the prophets, in these last days, he spoke to us through a son, whom he made heir of all things and through whom he created the universe, who is the refulgence of his glory, the very imprint of his being, and who sustains all things by his mighty word, when he had accomplished purification from sins, he took his seat at the right hand of the majesty on high, as far superior to the angels as the name he has inherited is more excellent than theirs.

In short, God's voice is Jesus, the Lord of the Universe. So, the voice of God as it echoes throughout the ages is the voice of Jesus in history and in faith. For better reading of the connection between the voice of Jesus and the voice of God, one is referred to the sixth chapter of the Gospel of John where John demonstrates the divine exchange of the work of the Father through the Son (Jn 6:19-40). When it comes to the voice of God and discernment, a person who hears the voice of Jesus and abides by it is like someone who has built a house on a solid foundation, and no amount of wind or storm of life can destroy it. The voice of Jesus comes with power and authority because in it lies our hopes, our aspirations, our goals, and our being. A candidate discerning to the priesthood must therefore watch the voice of Jesus through the Church (his bishop, vocation director, formators, spiritual director, pastors) and those connected with the process of training to the priesthood. A candidate who enters the seminary with the presumption of being already formed should not proceed or be encouraged to pursue seminary training because he has 'the hardened heart' already and would not be open to formation. Other secular vocations might be appropriate for such candidates.

During the process of discernment, the voice of God is heard through mediation of the agents of vocations in the dioceses called the vocation director. A candidate who feels he is called to the priesthood may approach the diocesan vocation director to make his intentions known. At this moment, the voices the candidate may be hearing may be confusing, disturbing, mysterious, and direct. The first approach to discernment is to "ask" questions about the meaning of the call, and why the candidate feels he is being called at this moment? The second approach is to "seek," that is to make hard enquiries to the right personnel at the Chancery through his pastor or by attending workshops, seminars, etc., during the vocation drive. The third approach is to "knock," that is to make a commitment to attend interviews, fill out the application forms, and get ready for the training in the house of formation. Following the process is part of the formation and part of the discernment and, evidently, responding to the voice of God.

Candidates who are selected to the priesthood do have various ideas about the seminary-formation. They come to the seminary with this naïve idea that they are all formed, trained, educated, well-behaved, disciplined, and "ready to go". Some do not realize that, with the speed of enthusiasm perhaps 70 miles per hour, they are heading to a formation house that is operating at the speed of 20 miles per hour. The "seemingly" slow process called gradualism is what makes seminary formation special and what makes the training to the priesthood last so long. The Church in her wisdom made it so, so that training would endure and be fruitful and beneficial for selfless service to the Church and humanity.

The voice of God filters in through the whole process of discernment from the time of the propaedeutic year through the time of discipleship. The voice of God accompanies the candidate through the time of decision-process to the time when He finally subdues his will to the will of God. A vocation is fruitful when the will of the candidate synchronizes with the will of God, but sometimes it is not glaring. It is also mixed up with other voices, the self, the voice of the devil, or even the voice of the world. The moment the candidate experiences crisis (indecision, temptation, distractions, spiritual emptiness) is a moment where the grace of God will shed light and, with faith and courage, the candidate may overcome the difficulty by relying on the work of the Holy Spirit.

An analogy of the crisis of vocation may be gleaned from the story of the fall of our first parents Adam and Eve. This story involved God, the devil, Adam and Eve, and the garden of Eden. The voice of the devil sounds like this "Did God really tell you not to eat from any of the trees in the garden?" Watch the emphasis that the devil put on "really" and "from any of the trees" and observe how provocative that question is. Look at the voice of God through Eve: "We may eat of the fruit of the trees in the garden; it is only about the fruit of the tree in the middle of the garden that God said, 'You shall not eat it or even touch it lest you die.'" Watch again the location of this tree, "the middle of the garden." This tree must be "special." Only God knows what this tree is made of. Watch again, the voice of the devil and his interpretation of the meaning of this tree. "You certainly will not die." "God knows well that the moment you eat of it your eyes will be opened and you will be like gods who know what is good and what is bad."

Here, Eve was to make a choice of her life either to reject the devil's insinuations and remain in the garden or accept it and face the consequences. Eve listened to her own voice, listened to the voice of the devil, and saw the tree in the middle of garden (the world) and had to eat the "forbidden fruit." In all events in life, the voice of God is sometimes challenged, obstructed by the voice of self, the devil, and the world. If you juxtapose this story to that of the temptation of Jesus in the New Testament, the whole dynamics changes because Jesus knows the limitations of the devil, the limitations of self and that of the world. Jesus was tempted on three levels, his basic human needs, his power, and his allegiance. He defeated the devil outrightly by saying "not by bread alone," not by ostentatiousness (showoffs), but by complete allegiance to the will of God.

The devil had no choice but to depart from Him, and the Angels came to worship him.

In the story of Cain and his brother Abel, Cain heard the voice of God saying "Why are you so resentful and crestfallen? If you do well, you can hold up your head; but if not, sin is a demon lurking at the door: his urge is toward you, yet you can be his master." Cain ignored the voice of God and took his brother outside in the field and murdered him out of envy, jealousy, and pride. When God asked him, "Where is your brother Abel?" he said, "I do not know. Am I my brother's keeper?" The rest of the story ends with God cursing Cain for the rest of his life. The moral of this story shows that following God's voice leads to life, and ignoring Gods voice may lead to damnation.

Another classical example of the voice of God is when Eli in (I Samuel: 3:1-19) teaches Samuel how to pray. "Speak Lord, for your servant is listening." In this phrase, there is a clear disposition of the person praying that God is Lord and mighty, or there is clear obedience to God's voice and obvious readiness to absorb the action of God through active listening. Many candidates to the priesthood know how to pray (the rosary, the liturgy of the hours, adorations, and responses at Masses), but very few know how to listen to the voice of God in prayer. We have lost the art of prayer simply because we have lost the art of listening. The world does not listen anymore. One cannot discern the voice of God in life unless one has the skills of listening. The revelation of God to Samuel was not an easy task. Samuel believed that it was a human voice until Eli told him to stay still and overcome the fear and anxiety of the call. He was in the temple in adoration, perhaps meditating, but when he disposed himself to listen to the voice of God as was directed by Eli, then God spoke to him personally. Whatever God told Samuel was for the common good of the people of Israel, and Samuel did not hide anything to himself, but shared it with Eli.

The key word here is listening actively to the voice of God. "By listening to God through prayer, meditation, and worship, the Holy Spirit will begin to speak to you, revealing God's personal and timely word for your life" (Shirer, *Discerning the Voice of God*, p.185). Why is listening so important in our lives? Because prayer is never complete unless you listen to the other end. Prayer starts with me ("*a quo*"), but it is aimed at a goal ("*ad quem*"). It is only when we listen actively to the other end of prayer, that we begin to appreciate the goal of prayer. Our prayer does not change God, but it changes us to be better, to love more, to care more, to touch more lives, and to be more effective in the society. It is when we listen well that we will understand, and when we "stand-under" someone, the true meaning of obedience (o*b-udire*, to hear) comes with both insight and clarity.

Solomon is regarded as a wise man because he chose from the options God gave him, namely wealth, power, knowledge, and wisdom. He chose wisdom because to be a child of God, one must understand and obey the voice of God. He knew that power and wealth are earthly trappings that may eventually lead one astray, but he chose wisdom to understand what power and wealth mean in the context of the rulership of God. He did not choose knowledge because acquired knowledge is also transient and may disappear with time and circumstances. He chose wisdom as to make a right judgment on things of this world as they relate to God. He chose well because wisdom means the right path to pursue truth and God.

The prophets heard the voice of God in different occasions and spoke on his behalf. Many of them, like Ezekiel and Jeremiah, were challenged by their respective callings. Jeremiah, at one point, accused God of "duping" him. God used his human skills for a purpose, that is, to speak to his audience about the need to obey the laws of God and to avoid an impending danger. Ezekiel restored hope where there was hopelessness, assuring his audience that if they have faith in God, they will witness "the dead bones" coming back to life once more.

Most of these prophets were men of hope and reassurance of God's fidelity to the covenant. Isaiah, indeed, prophesied that a virgin shall conceive and bear a son and that his name will be called "Emmanuel" (God with us). Whether his audience understood that this will come to pass and be fulfilled in Jesus is another mystery in God's plan, but it did happen. The voice of God became the word of God. The word of God took flesh and dwelt among us. In summary, the voice of God is fruitful when we listen and act upon it as directed by the Holy Spirit.

A candidate searching for the voice of God must kneel in silent prayer and reflect through active listening the direction which God is leading him. If he "discerns in," and that decision is consistent with the will of God, well and good. But if he "discerns out," and that is what God wants for him in life, it is equally good. One is never a failure if he "discerns out" of a house of formation. There are great men and women who have lived outside a house of formation who are fulfilled and accomplished in life. "Be not afraid" as Saint Pope John Paul II always said.

Chapter 3

The Voice of the Devil

Now, let us consider what the voice of the devil sounds like. The voice of the devil sounds like the voice of the world with all its trappings, deceit, disguise, and cunning techniques. The real meaning of the devil is explained by the Spanish word "El diabolo" which means someone who throws confusion between two people—someone who brings obstacle in between persons, things, or ideas just to confuse, mislead, obstruct, destroy, damage, harm, kill and obvert the truth. The aim of the devil is to lie against God. The devil is a liar *par excellence*. The devil is a person who throws confusion between God and Man as in the case of our first parents. He throws confusion between man and man as in the case of Cain and his brother, Abel. He throws confusion between man and his fellow men and women as in the case between Moses and the people of Israel on their journey to the promised land. The voice of the devil comes to us through mediation, humans, things, and ideas. But the endgame is to mislead, destroy, damage, confuse, and malign the good work of God in the world.

When the candidate to the priesthood is discerning, the initial voice of the devil comes through feelings of unworthiness, past life experiences, failures in life, human weakness, Sin, and the sense of guilt. The devil's first attempt is creating doubt on the candidate's mind so that the candidate will have a double mind. When God is calling one, he knows one's strengths and weakness, but he calls anyway. What is required of the candidate is openness, trust, and docility to the voice of God. The devil always comes with these questions, "Who told you?" or "What do you mean?" or "Where are you now?" "What are you planning to do next?" "Why do you want to do it this way?" and "Are you sure you want to do this?" These questions are means to provide alternatives or opposite answers to what God intends one to do.

My advice to my students is to "focus your eye on the ball" (your call). Do not drop the ball. A good example is the dynamics between the devil and Jesus. The devil asks Jesus, "If you are the son of God, turn these stones into bread," knowing that Jesus has fasted for forty days and forty nights and is hungry. Jesus' response is, "It is not on bread alone that man survives, one can survive through the power of the word of God." The devil can put confusion into vulnerable minds just to create doubt and uncertainty in about every situation. The voice of the devil is heard through material things that are attractive to the senses like food, safety needs, relationships, and encounters with the material world. He uses the opportunity to provide negative thoughts about things, ideas, and people. The aim is to disrupt God's plan for the candidate.

The devil approaches humanity on three basic levels, the first is the physical, the second is the spiritual, and the third is the vocational (cf., Morgan, *The Voice of the Devil*, pp. 38-39). A candidate for the priesthood must therefore be watchful over his physical human body, his spiritual sanity, and his calling. The devil attacks these levels with every possible skill to disrupt, confuse, and oppose the designed plan of God. The voice of the devil appeals to our concupiscence, especially what we see, touch, hear and taste. Because these things are attractive and desirable to the senses, we tend to give in to them easily. How many times have we been tempted through our eyes by what we see and watch every day through the television and social media, and what are the challenges we face in resisting them? How many times have we doubted the presence of God in our lives because the devil has encouraged us to doubt and to fear the unknown? How many times have we been distracted from our studies or prayers because the devil is putting confusing ideas in our heads?

A disciplined candidate who is discerning must carefully watch the proper use of the senses, the head, and the heart to overcome the pranks of the devil. The voice of the devil is heard loudly through the social media outlets like phones, computers, television, and newspapers. Imagine fifty years ago when social media was not dominant in society, there was less promiscuity and pornographic revolution than what we currently have. It seems to me that the more we claim to advance in education, science, and technology, the more backwards we move in terms of morality and behavior modification. The higher the technology, the more the devil advances in the use of them to confuse, distract, and upset the plan of God.

Phones have been a great asset of easy and handy communication throughout the world, but they have been the cause of broken families and relationships. Teenagers and young adults many times misuse phones by getting addicted to them, watching images that defile the integrity of their human person. The same could be said for television and computers in our homes and offices. The devil will always rejoice when these objects are misused. One of the dangers of the spread of social media is the breaking of nuclear families. Watch families going out for dinner. At the table, everybody has a phone. Family members are so concerned about their phones that the simple courtesy of family socialization is absent. Children, throughout dinner time, engage in frivolous conversation with their friends and not with the immediate family. Meals are eaten devoid of family contact and healthy dynamics. When the bond that holds families is broken, there is no amount of counseling or psychiatric consultation that will remedy the situation. Sometimes, the damage is discovered a day too late.

The book of James points out that the cause of division, or what he calls war in the family, is the abuse of human passion (James 4:1-6) The love of self and the world translates into the love of the devil. James says, "Submit yourselves to God. Resist the devil, and he will flee from you." Now let us consider the voice of the world in a more detailed fashion.

Chapter 4

The Voice of the World

What God created is good. He found that all he has done in the world is good but along the line, something extra ordinarily happened. Man and woman fell and ran short of the mercy of God. The consequence of this failure was suffering, pain, poverty, hard labor, and death. So, the voice of the world is a mixture of the good, the bad, and the ugly. Most often, what people hear loudly and clearly is the sound of what is bad and ugly and less and less of what is good in the world. A cursory look at the faith development of the ancient people shows how God made the initial call of man and woman and how this call was distorted by disobedience and neglect. He called again through Abraham Jacob and Moses. He provided them with his commandments. Their faith remained fickle to the point where they doubted their leaders. He provided them with judges, kings, and prophets, and they dishonored some and killed some. Because of their infidelity, they were divided and separated from one another.

God sent his own son—some believed him, some ignored him, and some killed him, but he rose again as scripture says. The church was founded on the faith of the risen Lord through the Apostles. Some of the apostles were men of little faith, and Jesus reminded them many times, "Do not be afraid." Philip and Thomas were known to be doubters, but they hung in with little faith in the risen Lord. They carried the mission to the world that was accessible to them. Most of them died by crucifixion. That churches are spread all over the world is empirical evidence of belief in the risen Christ. But what the church is doing and where it is going is diametrically opposed to the voice of the world today. Few examples are necessary here. Based on facts before the author, the church is preaching that the "kingdom" is where God is (Heaven), whereas the voice of the world is saying, "This kingdom is here on earth." The church will sing, "seek you first the kingdom of heaven, and the rest will be given to you," but the world is saying, "explore and harvest this world to its fulness and let's see what happens next."

Wise men and women of the past, both secular and religious, have poured ideas in writing on the best approach of pursuing knowledge and God. "Everyone desires to know," says one wise man, but to know what? While some have focused on the process of knowing, others have searched for the object of knowledge. At the beginning of the search for truth or God, some wiser men veered into arguments as to whether this God exists. Thomas Aquinas provided five ways of God's existence, but his ideas are not satisfactory to today's thinkers. There arose so many "isms" in philosophy and theology that today the voice of the world is more confused about itself, its creator, and the essential values and meaning of life itself. It appears clear that the world is surrendering itself to secularism—an ideology which believes that the world is supreme and whatever happens here ends here.

Secularism, a term used for the first time around 1846 to the American audience, was not new. It has been there from the beginning when our parents chose the devil in place of God. There was a time when there was absolute truth, and absolute truth was identified to subsist in the supreme being of all religions. Things fell apart. There is this zig-zag movement of the importance of reason over faith or over spiritual life, and then the autonomy of reason itself. "The world has come of age," some would say, therefore, whatever is not earthly, or worldly, must be cast away. Thus, there arose a sequence of thinking (rationalism, empiricism, existentialism, pragmatism, secularism, and relativism) that combined to confuse the already confused world.

When we hear the voice of the world today, we must be careful to discern from what ideological lens the voice is coming. Joseph Cardinal Ratzinger asserts that "there is a primary stumbling block to belief. The distance between the visible and invisible, between God and Not-God, is concealed and blocked by the secondary stumbling block of Then and Now, by the antithesis between tradition and progress, by the loyalty to yesterday that belief seems to include." There is this idea that the past is gone and given way to the present and that looking at the future is more progressive and fulfilling, but we tend to forget that the God whom Jesus revealed to us is the God of yesterday, today, and forever.

The voice of the world has in it also the voice of God. This voice comes through mediation of the church, the messengers of God, men, and women of good will, and those faithful to the Church militant. For the past three hundred years, the voice of the world that seems to overshadow all voices emanates from the theory of Darwinism which teaches that man descended from the Ape—a belief which negates God as the creator and author of the universe. This theory planted the seed of the separation between the secular and the spiritual. Over the years, the threat of secularism which originated from Darwinism

metamorphosed into communist ideology which prohib-
its any form of religion. Thus, Darwinism negates God, the
human soul, the afterlife.

Into this vacuum (religionless society), communism
enters as the be-all and end-all, creating an intellectual slav-
ery (Cuthbert, *The Surrender to Secularism*, p. 12). These
atheistic ideologies, namely Darwinism, communism, secularism, gave rise to liberalism. Today, we have the threat
of relativism or total indifference to religious values. In such
a world, the candidate to the priesthood finds himself en-
meshed amidst a confusion where pleasure is venerated in
place of discipline, joy and happiness are preferred in place
of pain and suffering, the sense of the sacred is ignored and
perhaps viewed as superstitious, and morality is taught as
ethics without religious education and spirituality. As far
back as 1952, the U.S. Bishops warned about the dangers of
secularism. As the State was separated from the Church,
liberalism presented atheistic demands, namely, "that all
religious teaching in public schools and the use of the Bible
be prohibited; that the theological oath in all departments
of government and courts of the land be abolished; that the
laws looking towards the enforcement of Christian morality be abrogated" (op. cit, p.14). With these kinds of policies
in public and many private schools, society becomes

religionless, and atheism becomes entrenched in families and in society at large. This is the background from which the present candidates are recruited to the formation houses. With this background, students are already so inundated with atheistic environments and secular mindsets that it becomes extremely difficult to figure out their genuine intentions during the process of vocation interviews.

The voice of the world with which they are acquainted becomes the voice of social media through phones, computers, television, Facebook, Twitter, Instagram, and all the technological innovations of the day. Who knows what will happen next? Perhaps the threats of Artificial Intelligence (A.I.) will add its own challenges to the already complicated mess of atheism and secularism. What impact do these atheistic secularities have on the family? There is a belief out there that the family is at war with the threat of social media in terms of the contents of what young people are allowed or not allowed to view.

Many young people today know too much above what they are required to know through phones and television. The increase of gun violence and suicidal incidents point to the fact that the young people are being self-trained to maladaptive behavior through social media. On religious grounds, the faith development of young people in general is not solid enough to carry them through adult life. In many schools, religion is not given a priority. With this background, candidates aspiring to the first level of formation, called propaedeutic in church terms, must start with the preliminary basics of faith like meaning of the articles of faith, the creed, the introduction to the Bible, the formative factors of theology, like reason and belief; the teachings of the documents of the Second Vatican Council, the essential elements of the sacraments, the commandments, and the importance of prayer in Christian life. The guiding principle here is to remember what Jesus said to the disciples, "You are in the world, but you are not of the world."

The candidate who is serious in discernment to the priesthood should know that he belongs to the world whose voice is contrary to the voice of God he is aspiring to hear and must make a categorical decision to ignore the voice of self, the devil, and the world in order to pursue the voice of God. "Come Holy Spirit fill the hearts of the faithful and enkindle in them the fire of your love." Amen.

Conclusion

The place to acquire holiness in the real sense of the term is the seminary. A Seminarian who seeks priestly virtues (obedience, chastity, celibacy, pastoral charity, to mention but a few) will learn them in the seminary. If one is not a holy seminarian, it will be difficult to become a holy priest. What the church needs today is a holy priest, not a magician, a ritualist, a wonder worker, a mega-church leader, a super-administrator, a future-campaign fundraiser, or a lazy priest. A good priest is a holy priest, and a holy priest is the ideal priest who is attracted by the people of God. Therefore, select the voices you hear every day while in the seminary, whether you are in the chapel or classrooms or sports room. "When you hear his voice today, harden not your hearts."

Books Referenced or Consulted

The Catholic Edition of the Bible (OT and NT)

Campbell, Morgan G. (1978). *The Voice of the Devil.* Baker book house Grand Rapids, Michigan.

O'Gara M., Cuthbert, C.P. (Bishop of Yuan- ling). (1978). *The Surrender to Secularism.* St. Louis, Missouri: Cardinal Mindszenty Foundation, Inc.

Powell, John, S.J. (1969). *Why am I afraid to tell you who I am?* Allen, Texas: Tabor Publishing,

Ratzinger, Joseph Cardinal. (1968). *Introduction to Christianity.* San Francisco, California: Ignatius Press.

Shirer, Priscilla. (2017). *Discerning the Voice of God.* Nashville, Tennessee: Life Way Press.

About the Author

Rev. Eugene Azorji is a Catholic priest of the Diocese of Ahiara in Nigeria currently on a mission in the Diocese of Dallas, Texas. He was the pioneer rector of Seat of Wisdom major seminary Ariam in Umuahia diocese. He is currently the resident spiritual director at Holy Trinity Seminary in Dallas, Texas. He has a doctorate in Dogmatic theology from the Pontifical Urban University in Rome and a master's in education from St John's University New York. He was ordained a priest in 1980 and has served as a formator, teacher, and spiritual director for over thirty years. He is the author of *Why do Priests and Religious Die Young. The Voices We Hear Daily* is the latest of his publications.

www.ingramcontent.com/pod-product-compliance
Lightning Source LLC
Chambersburg PA
CBHW072039060426
42449CB00010BA/2353